What If?

To Eloise Hooper
Blessings!
Ken Brown   Aug., 2019

What If?

*A Collection of First-Person,
New Testament Sermons*

BY KENNETH F. BROWN

Foreword by Randy A. Marshall

RESOURCE *Publications* · Eugene, Oregon

WHAT IF?
A Collection of First-Person, New Testament Sermons

Resource Publications
An Imprint of Wipf and Stock Publishers
199 W. 8th Ave., Suite 3
Eugene, OR 97401

www.wipfandstock.com

PAPERBACK ISBN: 978-1-5326-8918-5
HARDCOVER ISBN: 978-1-5326-8919-2
EBOOK ISBN: 978-1-5326-8920-8

Manufactured in the U.S.A.   04/18/19

This tiny volume is dedicated to the One who gave His life to make such stories possible and to my beautiful wife and family who have encouraged me to share them.

Contents

Acknowledgements

It is with boundless gratitude that I acknowledge the gracious and multifaceted editorial assistance of my lovely niece Sarah Johnson, and the encouragement and patience of my editor Matthew Wimer at Wipf and Stock to bring this project to fruition. Many friends and family members have contributed generously along the way, especially my talented grandchildren. Special thanks goes to Col. Randy Marshall for his generous comments in the Preface. And finally, appreciation is extended to all those who have received these efforts with encouraging comments and receptive hearts.

Foreword

By Randy A. Marshall, Ch., Col., USAF

I have never been to the Holy Land, but I have walked down the streets of Jerusalem a thousand times. I have never met a biblical character, but I count many as my friends. Through the Spirit-led lens of biblical interpretation and an active imagination, I have felt the Judean sun beat down upon my neck, tasted the sweet waters drawn from the well of Jacob, heard the booming voice of one proclaiming in the wilderness, wept at the foot of the cross, and rejoiced beside the empty tomb.

Over the years, I have found the Bible to be more than words on a page, more than a book of history, and more than a collection of devotional thoughts. The Bible, at its core, tells the powerful message of God's redemptive story. This centuries old, dramatic narrative includes men and women from all walks of life with various personalities and diverse worldviews.

One of the great pleasures of biblical exploration is to step into the sandals of these men and women and walk where they walked—experiencing each sight, sound, taste, and touch along the way. Spiritual guides are needed in order to properly navigate this divinely imaginative journey. For me, at the top of the spiritual guide list is my friend and mentor, Ken Brown.

Ken profoundly thinks as a trained theologian, painstakingly prepares as a skilled craftsman, and lovingly communicates as a lifelong pastor. He has significantly influenced my life. Any success I have had in over thirty years of serving as a local church pastor and United States Air Force chaplain is rooted in foundational truths taught and lived by this great man of God.

His sound, biblical, creative teaching instilled in me during my formative years has influenced me to this day. His sermons opened doors of understanding as the truth of the Word of God leapt from the page, touched my heart, and transformed my life. Along the way, I discovered biblical characters to be real men and women. They lived in a particular time and place and had distinctly human characteristics common to every age. Personally identifying with them, even now, allows me to see myself more clearly and realize that I am part of God's redemptive story as well.

Both in biblical times and today, when everyday people are exposed to the light of God's truth, they exhibit a variety of emotional, mental, physical, and spiritual responses. Some, though initially fearful, embrace the Good News. Others, though feeling spiritually inadequate, joyfully celebrate as they receive God's grace and mercy. Incredibly, there are also individuals who, despite being provided the brightest of lights, remain frustratingly determined to dwell in the darkness.

Ken Brown's "what if" first-person narratives give an insider look at a variety of New Testament biblical characters and their personal responses to the light of divine revelation. These personal journals—expressing an intimate perspective, combining the biblical account with known archeological, cultural, and political facts interspersed with imaginative thought—provide a dramatic story that illustrates and illuminates powerful truth. These stories can enhance our biblical exploration as we take a behind-the-scenes look at some of our favorite or not-so-favorite biblical characters. By following the lead of spiritual guides God has put in our path—such as the Ken Browns of the world—we can discover and rediscover biblical personalities at their best, and worst.

Through the illuminating power of the Holy Spirit, these men and women still speak to us today, inspiring and enriching us in our spiritual walk. Listen to them. Learn from them. Get to know them. Through this eye-opening, heart-transforming journey, may your life be enriched, and may you also discover that though you have never met a biblical character, you can count many as your friends.

Introduction

These "stories" may be thought of as sermons or messages or homilies. They developed over the nearly fifty years of pastoral ministry that occupied my life. In an effort to make the biblical narratives that are repeated so often at Christmas and Easter and other special occasions more enjoyable, I sometimes resorted to "stories."

Imagination plays a great part, but I have tried to stay as close to the biblical basis as possible in each story. Using a "what if" approach, I tried to develop storylines that would elicit interest, suspense, and a spiritual conclusion. I especially hoped to capture the attention of younger listeners, who always enjoy a story. Whether I succeeded in any fashion is debatable, but some friends and family thought these "stories" worthwhile. It is always intriguing to image how Peter might have reacted or the shepherds responded.

"What if" we could have been an insider to some of the greatest stories ever told?

Kenneth F. Brown
November 2018

That Night

Luke 2:1–20

That night was not nearly so cold as most nights had been that winter, and the heavy, late rains had stopped suddenly four days previously. Elihu, my grandfather, had called our attention to the strangeness of the week, and as the elder in our camp, he thought it significant. Abdon and I listened with all due respect and promptly forgot about it. Later on, we would remember these little things and say knowingly to each other, *"Adonai etzer."* "The Lord was helping." It is so much easier to travel when there is no rain.

For days, the roads had been full of people coming and going for the census.

From Migdal Eder, the tower of the flock, we watched the groups moving down the hill from Bethlehem, heading north out of the valley, toward Jerusalem. We saw others coming over the hills from Jerusalem to climb the long slopes to Bethlehem until the town was filled with visitors. Only at night did the traffic stop, and we sat around our campfire talking about the many strangers in our little village.

My people had been shepherds for nearly two hundred years. It was a mean job. Common sense called it low-down work, and men who did it were regarded as trash. But we were no ordinary shepherds. My forefathers fought for Israel's freedom under "the Hammer" John Hyrcanus, and so to my family came the honor of keeping the sheep that were *kadoshim*, "dedicated" to God. They were destined to be sacrificed at the Temple services. We never were able to attend ourselves, but we were given special provision under the Law that we might be forgiven our absences. However, Grandfather Elihu made certain that we observed the holy days as best we could. He knew a great deal of Scripture from memory, and we were expected to learn it also. In fact, the Sabbath before that night, we had learned about a promise foretold by the prophet Micah. It was to gleam with the light of fulfillment:

> "But thou, Bethlehem Ephratah, though thou be little among the thousands of Judah, yet out of thee shall He come forth unto me that is to be the ruler of Israel, whose goings forth have been from of old, from everlasting."

Abdon, my cousin, was sixteen, and I was fifteen-and-a-half that winter. We had great fun together. He was the best shot with a sling that I ever knew, but he wasn't as good at tracking lost sheep as I was. He could whip me wrestling, but he wasn't nearly as good as I was at making reed flutes. We had plenty of time for play, since our flock was seldom bothered by jackals or wild dogs. In fact, our only real trouble was with two-legged jackals who tried to steal the sheep. Imagine stealing an animal that is kadosh, God's own possession. Except for moving the flocks, gathering wood, and trips into town to help father or Uncle Reuben with food supplies, we were not too busy. One job we didn't like was preparing a flock for the Jerusalem trip. Each sheep had to have the burrs removed from its fleece and be carefully examined for cuts and bruises.

I'm sorry, I must stop the family history and get on with the story.

That night started like a great many others. Nahor, my uncle, and Kemuel, my father, were taking the second watch. My grandfather, Elihu, was getting too old, really, for the long night watches, so he took the first watch and then slept until morning. Abdon and I were half awake. The sky was clear and the dark velvet of the heavens displayed every star at its best. The wood smoke smelled good mixed with the breeze, and we talked quietly. The warmth of our robes and the softness of the sheepskin pallet finally put us to sleep.

I awoke with a start as though someone had touched me. I listened—and heard only the distant barking of a dog. It was strangely still. I sat up and looked down the slope to see my father and Uncle Nahor. The sheep seemed restless. My father was looking first one way and then another like a man trying to decide which way to run. Then I saw it too. The glow of light grew brighter with every passing moment until it seemed the sun had invaded the night with its brilliance, lighting our whole hillside like day. A man appeared before my father—at least he looked like a man, but his presence hurt my eyes. His robe gleamed like sunlight on a new snow. He spoke in a voice majestic but exceedingly kind: "Do not be afraid."

He could have as easily asked me to fly to Jerusalem. It was then I realized my father was down on his knees and my uncle was prostrate on the ground. My own heart was pounding, and without knowing it, I had pulled my wool covering up to my eyes, and was peeking over the edge while my uncovered feet trembled from fright and from cold.

The angel, for that is who he was, continued speaking with a note of triumph in his voice: "Behold, I bring you good news of great joy. For unto you is born this day in the City of David the Savior who is Christ the Lord. You will find the baby wrapped in swaddling clothes and lying in a manger."

Suddenly beyond the gleaming light of the angel and the glory that surrounded us, we heard the blending of thousands of voices repeating over and over in beautiful music, "Glory to God in the highest, and peace on earth to men in whom He is well pleased." The grandeur took your breath away!

Then the voices grew dim, the light faded, the stars came back into view and the campfire coals glowed reassuringly. I thought to myself, "It was a dream."

Now, finally, I unfroze and was able to turn and see that Uncle Reuben was helping Grandfather to his feet. They were both rather pale and neither of them spoke. My father and Nahor had left the sheep and were coming very slowly up the slope. I looked beside me—Abdon had slept right through it all.

My father placed more wood on the fire, and as the flames leaped up, I saw the looks of bewilderment and astonishment on their faces. There was silence.

Then I realized my feet were nearly numb. I rearranged my covers and waited for Grandfather to speak. The old man trembled and his eyes sparkled and his voice was excited but firm. He had hoped to see the Messiah before death.

"Let us go immediately and find out what has really happened. We have a sign," Grandfather said, "and a promise. Let us see what God is doing."

Uncle Reuben said, "I agree, Father, but what of the sheep?"

"They are bedded—leave them to God. This matter is more important than all the sheep in Judah, my son."

Then everyone started to talk at the same time. "Did you see what I saw?" "Did you hear the voices?" "How many do you think there were?" "What a strange way to announce the Messiah." "How can a baby . . . ?"

I started to wake Abdon only to find that he was already peering from under his warm covers. He had a funny look on his face as though he couldn't believe his ears. "What," he demanded, "has happened that we are all leaving the sheep and going into town?"

"Get ready to go, and I will tell you on the way."

I wasn't really sure myself about everything, and as I told Abdon about the angels, my mind was running ahead. If it is true, then will there be a new day in Israel, a new life? Will freedom, happiness, peace, and prosperity abound? What a tremendous thing this would be.

Abdon was skeptical. "I can understand the part about the Messiah, the Savior, but you must have heard wrong about this baby. The Messiah is no infant!"

Bethlehem, the City of David, was about a mile away. I never before saw Grandfather walk so fast. The look of expectancy on his face seemed translated into his legs. Of course it was easy for us to keep up. How strange it felt to be going to town at this hour and on such an errand. The men were discussing the events as they walked, and were wondering where to begin the search for a new baby in a feed trough.

Abdon thought we were asking for trouble. "You know," he said to me, "that people think we're a bunch of bums anyway. Why would God bother to tell us anything about something as tremendous as the Messiah's coming? Can't you see us waking up old Ahimilech and popping the question to him, 'Where is he that is born King of the Jews? The angels have announced His coming to us. He is wrapped in banding cloths and sleeps in a manger.' You know what he'd say? 'You boys take these drunk old shepherds out of here before I call the centurion.' Ha!"

We reached the outskirts of the little town we knew so well. It was not really cold anymore, and the walk had warmed us. The starlight seemed especially bright. The men had decided that the largest stable was in back of the inn of Joash, and so we headed there. The inn sat just off the Jerusalem road, and the stable was built in part from a shallow cave in the hillside. Travelers' animals were cared for inside the stable.

It was still and quiet. As we approached, we saw lamplight gleaming. Two women left the stable talking in low tones. We slipped in and found a couple sitting beside a manger carved out of the cave's limestone wall—and on a bed of hay, wrapped in swaddling bands, we saw a brand-new baby sleeping in his unusual bed. The man and his wife smiled a welcome to us, and he greeted us in a happy voice, "*Shaloam.*"

Grandfather went down on his knees close to the manger, and with tears running down his face, he began to recite a favorite psalm:

> "Bless the Lord, O my soul, and forget not all His benefits; who forgiveth all thine inequities; who healed all thy diseases; who redeemeth thy life from destruction, who crowneth thee with loving kindness and tender mercies."

We crowded a little closer. It seemed strange, but somehow it felt right—we too knelt, and I thanked God for the little Messiah. My grandfather finished a prayer of thanksgiving and asked the baby's name. The young mother, hardly much older than Abdon and me, answered in such a glad and gracious way that no one thought it improper. "The angel said we must call him *Yeshua*, 'Savior,' for he will save his people from their sins."

Then Grandfather described to the couple what we had seen and heard earlier and what wonder filled our minds and what joy filled our hearts. We worshipped in quietness. We exchanged the old words with each other, but with new meaning: "Peace to you. Grace and peace to you."

With our hearts bursting with happiness, we began the long walk back to the sheepfold. Grandfather started singing a psalm, and we all joined in, setting the neighborhood dogs to howling. Should we tell our sleeping families? Later, at the fourth watch, we would tell the Good News. But anyone awake at that hour must have thought us drunk—and we *were* drunk, intoxicated with the glory of God and the grace of His coming into our lives to be our Savior.

We wondered how this baby could be our Redeemer. We could not then see the dreadful cross at Golgatha and the stone had still to be rolled from the Lord's tomb. But one thing we knew beyond a shadow of a doubt: the promises were coming true that night.

I wanted to sing with Isaiah:

> "Unto us a child is born and unto us a son is given; and the government shall be upon His shoulder; and His name shall be called Wonderful Counselor, the mighty God, the everlasting Father, the Prince of Peace."

That night he came not only into a lowly manger bed; He came forever into my heart and life.

Has he come into yours?

There in Bethlehem

Matthew 2:1–16

Shaloam lechem, peace to you. My name is Obed bar Elihu. My home is Bethlehem. In two weeks I will become a candidate for bar mitzvah, a son of the Law. I should not boast, but I have learned my lessons well, and my mother is almost finished with my tallit, my prayer shawl. It has long blue and white tassels, probably the nicest anywhere. Besides, I am the best runner in my synagogue class, and except for Joash, I am the best shot with a sling in the whole school. My father says it is because I come from a long line of shepherds— you know, they use their slings to guard their flocks.

But this is not what I must tell you. This strange story you will hardly believe. I would not have believed it myself, except that I was there. Nothing like it has happened since Solomon was king.

These unusual-looking men from somewhere in Persia came riding in. Wait—I am getting ahead of myself.

The story actually started weeks ago during the signing-up for taxes here in Bethlehem. The Romans were meddling again, my father says. People came from everywhere until the town was overflowing—thousands. Well, it looked like thousands to me! Anyway, there was a couple from up in Galilee, and the woman had a baby out in the stable in back of Abner's Inn. There was no room inside the inn. That was what really started this whole thing. All kinds of stories went around about this baby. He was supposed to be real special.

At least my uncle Boaz thought so. My uncle Boaz is still a shepherd. He cares for the *kadoshim*, the sheep used in sacrifice at the Temple. You should have heard what he told my father. I didn't hear it all; I was supposed to be asleep. But he talked about angels and light as bright as the sun—at midnight!—and beautiful music coming from heaven. He talked about how scared he was, how surprised they all were, how happy he was when he got to see the baby, how he felt in his own heart that this was God's Messiah. There was more, but I guess I fell asleep.

People in our village talked and argued. Our synagogue rabbi said that the baby couldn't possibly be the Messiah, because the Messiah would be a powerful king, like David.

Well, about three days after the people finished enrolling for their taxes, this man and his wife and the new baby moved into the house across from ours. The place had been vacant and needed repair. Fixing it allowed them to stay there, my father said. The man found some work with Perez, the carpenter. The poor old man could hardly see to do the work the people needed, and this new man was real good, helping him to catch up and all that. My mother told me the family had to stay here until the baby and his mother were strong enough to travel again.

So I went over and got to be friends with them. The man's name was Joseph bar Jacob, and his wife's name was Mary. Their home was in Nazareth.

The little boy was called Jesus, and he was pretty good for a baby. He didn't seem very special.

I carried water for them and helped them find out where to buy the best figs and olives in the market. Mother gave them some vegetables from our garden—they didn't have too much, I guess. Everything had just about settled down to normal, and these new folks were fitting in real well—they were even coming to the synagogue with us every Sabbath—until the day this group of strangers came riding into our village and upset the whole town.

I don't know who they were, but they had *some* fancy robes. Two of the men rode camels, and they were no ordinary camels. One was white all over—just beautiful. The other camel was dark-colored, nearly black. They had big fancy saddles and bridles, trimmed with real silver. My father said so.

Another of the leaders rode this tremendous white horse with a flowing mane and tail. The saddle and bridle had tassels and bells that jingled whenever he moved. I mean, they were something to see!

There were a number of others on camels and some servants on horses and donkeys carrying tents and water bags. The chief men were magi or wisemen.

They're supposed to have special wisdom and be real smart. To me, they just looked very old. They were dressed for traveling at first, but after finding the baby Jesus, they went out to the edge of town and set up camp. Then they came back dressed like kings—gold and purple, blue and silver, with tassels and embroidery and ornaments all over. Linen and silk, most of it was—my mother told me—you just never saw anything like it. I watched from our doorway but wanted to get closer so I could really see what was going on. I had a bright idea: I grabbed my water pot and ran to the well. Then I came back and pretended to water the camels so I could peek inside.

Mary was holding Jesus on her lap, and these wisemen were unwrapping some cloth from around their bundles. You should have *seen* the gold chest and this beautiful jar of perfume or something! And there was this little silver basket-kind-of-thing with holes in it and sweet smells coming out of it. The men laid their gifts at Mary's feet, and then they got down on their knees—right there on the dirt floor—and bowed down to the ground before the little Jesus. Boy, was I surprised! Uncle Boaz must be right, I thought.

About then, a camel nuzzled my ear, and I jumped up and left real fast for home. After a while, the men came out and talked with Joseph for a long time.

Sometimes they pointed up toward the sky, and sometimes they pointed east. The next morning they got on their animals, and the whole bunch started south toward Gaza. I thought they would head back to Jerusalem.

My father talked with Joseph also, and I think he was convinced that the baby was really special—that he was the long-promised Messiah. He and mother talked about it often in the weeks after, especially how his name meant "savior," *Yeshua.*

Two days after the wisemen left, Joseph and Mary packed up the baby and their things. They bought a donkey with some money from the wisemen, I guess. Anyway, all at once they were gone. The next day the most terrible thing I know happened.

A big bunch of soldiers from King Herod came down from Jerusalem, and before anyone could do anything, they began to kill the little boys and babies in our village, and even out in the country around us. It was terrible and sad.

Everyone cried and cried for days. I was surely glad that Jesus was gone. And then I wondered—did they know something bad was about to happen? I guess God needed the special baby to grow up. I thought about it two or three days after all the funerals, and then I forgot it. My bar mitzvah kept me pretty busy.

[Pause]

Shaloam ammi, peace, my people. My name is Obed, Son of Elihu. My home is Bethlehem. I have lived thirty years since I first told you my strange story concerning a baby named Jesus and some peculiar wisemen who came to worship Him. Much has happened, and much I have learned since that unusual time.

I have come lately from Jerusalem. I know now why the Christ child escaped from Herod so many years ago. God had another time for him to die. I do not understand it all, but I saw him nailed to a Roman cross just outside David's city. That was two days ago, and now I wait, sorrowing, to hear from his disciples. James, the Son of Zebedee, an old friend of mine, will bring me word this Sunday afternoon. We had hoped that it was Jesus who should redeem Israel and bring salvation to this dark world.

We had hoped.

Surely this cannot be the end.

In your heart, do you feel that this could be *the end*?

Little Girl, Wake Up!

Luke 8:40–56

Let me tell you about what happened here in the city of Capernaum one morning a few years ago. On the very morning that the Gadarene demoniac was so amazingly healed, fear and dismay intensified in a family home on the other side of the city.

As the sun came breaking through early morning shadows, the narrow city streets filled with the everyday sounds of a Roman officer drilling his garrison beside the fort, the barking of dogs, squawking of chickens, calls of peddlers, bits of family conversations, and children's squabbles.

But in one house in the Jewish quarter, everything was hushed. People tiptoed and spoke in whispers. In a little bedroom, a father and mother knelt beside a small bed. Their daughter, just twelve years old, lay there, inert and unresponsive. All through the night they had watched, hoping against hope, fighting their fears, their resentments, their bewilderment. Why should she be so ill?

Now the new day had dawned, and sunlight flooded the room and fell on the pale, drawn face of the young girl—and their hope vanished with the night. No doctor was needed to tell them their little girl was dying. The ache in their hearts was overwhelming. Despair crushed them. Tears flowed.

The father's name was Jairus. He was the leading elder in the Capernaum synagogue. His reputation was unblemished, his righteousness unquestioned in the community. He was a spiritually sensitive man, a deep thinker, and he cherished the hope of Israel that the Messiah might come. He had heard Jesus teach and interpret the scriptures. He had talked with Jared the demon-possessed, and Machir the paralytic, who had both experienced the healing touch of Jesus. He had seen miracles with his own eyes, and rejoiced at the spiritual wholeness the young teacher imparted. A conviction had grown in Jairus's heart that Jesus was the Anointed One, God's Savior for his people—but the kind carpenter was very different from what he had expected, and from what the rabbis expected too.

Then, as illness struck his daughter, Jairus forgot his speculations about the young teacher.

As he waited beside the bed of his child, listening to her labored, shallow breathing, he realized that he was no longer praying. With a guilty start, he began once more to turn his mind to God, to beg, to implore mercy—but no words of prayer came. Instead, an idea slipped into his mind and became a heady impulse: "Get Jesus! Jesus could help. Jesus can heal. Jesus loves children."

He got up quickly, bent briefly to put his arms around his wife, and whispered, "I'm going to get Jesus. I'm sure he can help."

All but running, he left the house as servants and friends looked questioningly after him. "Where was he going now? Didn't he know she might die at any moment? Why didn't he stay with her? Who would comfort his wife?"

Jairus grabbed the first man he found on the streets. His excitement and agitated manner almost frightened the fellow. "Obed," he said, "have you seen Jesus of Nazareth? Do you know where he is? Tell me quickly!"

"Jairus! I don't know. He and his disciples went by boat to Gadara yesterday. I think he was trying to get away from the crowds for a while."

"Oh no! I've got to find him," cried Jairus. "Maybe they've come back. Thank you, Obed."

The ruler of the synagogue went running in the direction of the boat docks, his robes flapping in a very undignified manner. Obed started to call after him, to ask about his daughter's condition, but changed his mind, muttered a prayer, and went on his way.

Down at the beach, where the fishing boats were harbored, Jairus saw a crowd. "He must be here. He's got to be here," he gasped to himself, panting and heaving from the exertion.

He began threading his way through the crowd, to the annoyance of some, who choked on their harsh words when they recognized the intruder as their honored elder.

Then Jairus saw Jesus in the prow of a boat about to be landed. Jairus ran to the shore as the keel grated on the pebbles. Down he went at the feet of Jesus, imploring him to come and heal his daughter. The Savior calmed him, reassured him, listened to the torrent of need, and instantly began to move toward the city and Jairus's home.

The crowd moved with them, talking, jostling, with word of Jesus's errand spreading rapidly through the noisy multitude. Moving as quickly as possible in the throng, Jesus, Jairus, and the disciples started up the cobblestone main street. Peter, James, Andrew, and other disciples tried to form a circle around their master, both to protect and to run interference for him. The excitement of the crowd grew.

People shouted at each other, elbowed each other, and threatened each other. Frightened children and animals scooted for cover in doorways along the street. Dust hovered over the whole noisy scene.

Then all at once, the entire quivering mass slid to a halt. People tripped over each other and bumped into one another, some laughing and others cursing. "What's happening? What's going on? What's he doing now?"

A babble of voices arose over the mob that was now milling around as people tried to get a glimpse of Jesus. In the center of the jostling, with a frantic Jairus at his side, stood Jesus. The disciples looked questioningly at Jesus and at each other. Jesus always seemed so calm in the midst of bedlam—still in command. But why had he stopped?

In a quiet voice, Jesus, gazing around at the folk nearest, asked simply, "Who touched me?"

There was no answer.

In a sterner tone, Jesus repeated his question, "Who was it who touched me?"

Peter, in his usual fashion, opened his mouth at the wrong time: "Master, the way this crowd is pushing, lots of people have probably touched you. They didn't mean anything by it. C'mon let's get going."

Jesus just looked at Peter—a silent rebuke—and then said, "Someone touched me in a special way, for divine energy has been drawn from me."

The throng had quieted. Except for coughing and whispering and shuffling feet, the people were still and every ear was straining to hear, some tiptoeing to see.

All at once, with a great sob and gush of tears, a little shadow of a woman slipped into the circle and crumpled at Jesus's feet. In between sobs, she spilled out her story:

"O Lord, Rabbi Jesus, please forgive me for touching you. I've been sick with a hemorrhage for twelve long years. The physicians tried everything they could think of, but they couldn't help me. I went to every doctor I could find until I ran out of money. It just got worse. My husband divorced me, my family got tired of helping me, my friends gave up. I began to believe there was no hope for me and to long for death. But I heard about you; then I listened to you, and I'm so glad I did. I thought if I could just touch the tassel on your prayer shawl, I would be healed. With the crowd moving around you, I planned to slip in and touch the tassel and be gone before anyone even noticed."

Feeling ashamed and fearful of consequences, the tears started running down her cheeks again. Her gaunt face had brightened as she told her story, but now she was bewildered. Then she drew a deep breath and said firmly, "Lord, I know I'm well; you've healed me! O thank you, thank you." And she looked up at the Master to take whatever consequences were coming.

Jesus smiled tenderly at her, stretched out his hands to lift her, and said, "My daughter, your faith has healed you. *Shaloam lechem*—go in peace."

Once again, gratitude beamed from her radiant face. She whispered her thanks, her praise to God, and slipped back into the crowd. People seemed stunned at first—a path opened for the little woman. Then everyone began to talk again all at once, about the woman, about Jesus, about her amazing healing.

A servant slipped out of the crowd on the other side of the circle. He was scared and out of breath, and as Jesus turned to him, he spoke to Jairus: "Master, your daughter is dead. No use troubling the rabbi anymore." As the servant spoke, tears were streaming down his face.

Jairus moaned and covered his face with his hands. Jesus put his arm around the sobbing man's shoulders and said, "Do not be so frightened. Trust me, Jairus. Keep on believing, and she will be well again."

Turning to the crowd, Jesus instructed them to disperse, and his authority was immediately acknowledged. Some murmured and complained, but everyone began moving reluctantly in their different directions.

Jesus spoke tersely: "Peter, will you come with me, please? James, where are you? Yes, you too. And John, I want you too. The rest of you may come to the house later, but stay here for now."

With long, rapid strides, the Lord once more moved toward the elder's home. Jairus was beside him, the three disciples followed, and the family servant trailed behind, weeping copiously.

Before they had even passed through the gate and into the courtyard, the sound of wailing filled the air. Along with crying neighbors, friends, and relatives, the professional mourners had already started. Such shrieking and screaming was going on that one could hardly converse. Some servants and friends had thrown ashes on their heads and torn their robes to express their grief over the tragedy. The Lord, with a hurt look on his face, walked into the middle of all the commotion, and in a single great command, demanded silence.

Startled, everyone became silent. The paid mourners stopped their wailing.

Only the soft sounds of sobbing and sniffling continued.

Very emphatically, Jesus asked, "Why this crying and commotion? The child is not dead; she is only sleeping."

Some simply gaped in disbelief, but the professional mourners turned to each other, nodded their heads in derision, and began making snide remarks. "Sure she's asleep. We ought to be quiet so we don't wake her up. What a nap she's taking. He can't be serious. Who do you think you're kidding, fella? This is no time for jokes." They began laughing and ridiculing Jesus in a crude way. Behind their mockery was resentment that Jesus had interrupted their work.

Then the Master told them to go outside—politely, but firmly. They started to argue and fuss. Peter pushed one especially rude mourner toward the outer court. He swung at Peter, who ducked and then drew back his own fist, only to be restrained by James. A brawl was certainly not needed.

Jesus stepped between the disciples and the mourners, his eyes flashing. "Do as I say," he commanded, and this time the scowling group left, still muttering and threatening. Peter started to call something after them, and James stopped him again.

The bewildered elder and his wife waited in a corner of the room. Jesus went to them, took each gently by the hand, and asked to be shown to the daughter's bedroom. The disciples quietly followed. At the sight of the pale, still form, the mother began to cry again, and her husband tried to soothe and calm her while containing his own grief. Jesus, with Peter right behind him, went to the bed where the child was lying. The Lord paused, looking intently at the little girl. Her dark hair framed a lovely face, now drained of all color—the long curling lashes of her closed eyes rested on her white cheeks.

She does seem to be asleep, thought Peter. But she's not breathing. She's dead.

Jesus reached out and took the little hand, gripping it firmly between his big strong hands. Using the Aramaic of everyday conversation, he called to her as though he were waking her for breakfast: "*Talitha cum.*" "Little girl, wake up."

Her eyelids fluttered a moment, a great sigh signaled the return of breath, color rushed into her cheeks, and she sat up, smiling at the stranger who still held her hand, and smiled back reassuringly. Then Jesus helped her to her feet, and she walked unsteadily toward her stupefied parents, until they ran to hold her. Tears of joy, exclamations of praise to God, and thanks to Jesus alternated with their expressions of love and wonder. They were hardly able to believe it was true, that she was really alive again. Peter and John hugged each other, and Jairus exclaimed, "What did I tell you? He has done it again!"

Jesus finally got the attention of the rejoicing mother and father and gave them strict orders not to tell anyone what had happened. Then he suggested that they give their daughter something to eat so that her strength might be restored.

A servant who had slipped back into the hall of the house heard the daughter's voice reassuring her mother. Astonished at what she heard, she peeped into the bedroom and saw the young lady, very much alive, talking earnestly to Jesus. Practically flying out into the courtyard, she yelled the good news and was immediately surrounded by a skeptical crowd, eager to know what had happened. Was she really alive? How could it be? Questions flew back and forth.

Believers praised God and hoped to catch a glimpse of Jesus, who must surely be the Messiah. Doubters argued, posed explanations, or remarked about the sanity of the servant and the credibility of the carpenter.

But inside the kitchen, where a radiant twelve-year-old girl was taking care of a healthy appetite with bread, fish, raisins, and melon, there was joy, love, and gratitude to the Lord of Life, Jesus.

Do you know Him? Has He brought new life to you?

Failure

Mark 10:17–22

I was never so surprised, "stunned"—that's the word. Stunned. You just couldn't imagine that anything like that might happen. What a bright, hopeful morning that was. And then—then he failed. Unbelievable. Incredible. All those words.

I was still in a slow burn when the thing started. I was pouting—resentful—hurt. Seemed I was always having good intentions and then making a fool of myself. I had a lot to learn, dumb ol' me. As we had walked and talked since breakfast, we had moved further into the city. A group of young women laughing, gossiping, probably on their way to draw water, met us. A whole flock of children ran in circles around them. They were playing tag, I suppose, giggling, screaming, teasing.

The Master smiled when he saw them. Children always meant so much to him. That's where my mistake started.

Anyway, as we came up to this little crowd of mothers and kids, one of them recognized the Master and ran quickly to him, asking that he bless the baby that she held in her arms. Before we knew it, the whole bunch was on top of us. Each mother was clamoring for him to touch her child, and the older children kept on darting wildly in and out. They were typical peasants: not too clean, kind of ragged, not too smart. But he loved them.

It just seemed to me that the Lord shouldn't have to put up with all this disturbance. We had some very important things to talk about. The day before had been a real rough one for him. So

James and I began to gently—gently, mind you—push the women and those snotty-nosed kids away, just so he wouldn't be trampled or choked by the dust. That's when this lady-wrestler type shoved me back, and some inappropriate language was used.

The Lord said, "Stop it!" in that voice that means business.

I backed off. He looked right at me and said, "You must let little children come to me—never stop them, for the Kingdom of God belongs to such as these. In fact, I assure you that the man who does not accept the Kingdom of God like a little child will never get in."

I felt about that high. I was only trying to help, know what I mean?

By that time, it was as quiet as midnight, and the children began slipping over to the Master as he held out his arms to them. He really loved them, slobbery kisses and all. The lady-wrestler type smiled a "I told you so, dummy" look at me, and I began to study the ground at my feet. The bunch finally moved off with happy, backward glances, everybody talking at once. Two older boys thumbed their noses at me.

As I said, I was still fuming and feeling sorry for myself when this broke. I don't know where he came from, but all at once this young man came running in our direction. He had a couple of old servants behind him trying hard to keep up. One of them almost took a tumble when he tripped on his robe. Kind of funny, you know? Andrew snickered. At first I thought they were chasing the young fellow, but that wasn't the story at all. They belonged to him.

Well, this young guy came flying up and dropped on his knees in front of Jesus. What a sight that was! I knew before the dust had settled that this man was not exactly struggling for a living. You could look at his clothes and tell that. The beautiful purple dyes in that robe—it cost a bundle. There was this exquisite embroidery; needlework; that soft, white linen tunic; the tooled leather sandals and money bag; the velvet sash. The whole outfit yelled "filthy rich." The rings on his fingers and those soft hands were a dead giveaway. I bet he had never worked a day in his life. No dirt under his fingernails. His daddy must be one rich old man. But that's not so important. Well, as it turns out, it was.

There he knelt, getting all that finery dusty. He was good-looking too. He lifted his head and looked intently at the Master. "Good Teacher, tell me, please, what must I do to be sure of eternal life?"

The Lord looked at him and with a quick smile, he replied, "I wonder why you call me 'good.' No one is good—only God."

I thought to myself, that rich boy had better be careful with his words— unless he had sensed somehow that Jesus was indeed deity. I knew it, and a few others knew it, but I don't think Mr. Rich Man did.

Jesus never allowed you to think lightly of God. The whole matter of relating to His Father was much too serious to be superficial about it. You just don't play around with God where Jesus is concerned.

I recall the strange fear that gripped me the first time the Master came to our fishing camp. The beautiful goodness of God, the glory of his presence was in Jesus, and I couldn't even bear for him to get close to me. I was as sorry a sinner as ever drew breath, and yet he wanted to get right into my boat with me.

I'm sorry. Didn't mean to get off the track like that. But I don't believe this young man was really thinking about how awful goodness can be.

Anyway, we all waited to hear what the Master would say. His answer kind of surprised me really, because he knew right where that fellow was, and he met him on his own ground.

"You know the Commandments." That's what he said.

He had told us a hundred times that keeping laws, even the best, wouldn't save anybody—but that's what he said, because he knew that young man's mind. Believe me, that rich young man surely thought of himself as practically perfect.

And then Jesus got more specific: "Do not murder, do not commit adultery, do not steal, do not bear false witness, do not cheat, honor your father and mother."

Wow, I thought to myself, Lord, you know he hasn't had any trouble with those. He's never been mad enough to do a man in. I remembered the time I had nearly split Josiah's skull with an oar because he said I was lying about the size of my prize fish—this kid had never been hot like that.

And adultery? I don't think he was even married yet. What did he know of lust?

And steal? Why, he probably got enough allowance when he was growing up to feed my entire family. He never had to lie or cheat in school. All he had to do was study and play—no work for him. And you could tell he was smart just by looking at him.

What could he know about honoring his father and mother? He was spoiled rotten, I bet you.

Don't get me wrong. I'm sure he was a nice guy.

And then I nearly made a terrible mistake. I started to say, "Lord, you've left out the most important commandments. Ask him about God." But I bit my lip and, for once, kept my mouth shut.

The young man spoke up immediately, like I knew he would. "Master, I have carefully kept all these commands since I was quite young."

Then Jesus looked right into his insides, and I could tell by the expression on Jesus's face that he loved that youngster, that he wanted him for his own. I tell you, it was quiet and tense. You could feel God zeroing in.

The young fellow looked imploringly at the Lord as if to say: "There must be something else. I still don't have life. God doesn't give me any peace—any joy. There is no purpose, no meaning to my life."

I thought, "Now he's going to tell him. Now he's going to spell it out for him. Get ready, kid."

The Lord said, "You still lack one thing."

There was a long pause, and the man looked at the Lord expectantly.

Jesus said ever so quietly and firmly, "Go and sell everything you own. Give the money away to the poor—you will have wealth in heaven. And then come back and walk my road with me."

That's when the incredible, unbelievable happened. Such a look of agony came over that man's face as I have never seen. You could tell that he was fighting a tremendous battle. He wanted desperately to follow Jesus, but he had so many good things of his own. I realized then why the Master hadn't mentioned those first Commandments. This man was breaking them all. His wealth came first. His luxury and comfort were his gods. His pride sat like a great idol on the throne of his heart. He was totally bound by his self-indulgent way of life.

It was sinking in now. The message had gotten through, but the man was ruled by his possessions. He got to one knee slowly, and then, shaking his head, all but jumped to his feet. His face bore signs of confusion and resentment and shame, all mixed. But the battle was lost. He turned quickly and strode off. Then he broke into a run, his robe flying and his funny old servants hobbling after him. The young man was gone.

I half expected the Master to call him back, to urge him to reconsider. But he said nothing. I started to go after him myself, but my feet wouldn't move. He had been so near the Kingdom—and what a wonderful disciple he could be! I watched him disappear from sight and turned to question the Lord.

I was amazed. With all that miraculous power, he had failed. I'd seen him stop storms with a word, give sight to blind eyes, hearing to the deaf. I watched in wonder as he stopped a funeral and called a man back to life. Why couldn't he win this time?

Even as I thought it, I knew why. How carefully he guarded our freedom to choose. How anxiously he waited for us to respond in love and personal trust. How patient he had always been with me, dumb ol' me.

I looked at him there. He was still gazing at the corner where the young man had disappeared from sight. The defeated, grieving face was streaked with tears.

His lips trembled and those wondrous eyes closed in prayer—for a young man who said no to the only One who really matters.

Don't reject his love. Don't miss life's grandest blessing. Take it from someone who's been there. Three times Jesus asked me: "Peter, do you really love me?"

Come all the way with Him, regardless of the cost. Don't grieve the heart of God.

Journey into Light

John 9

I remember—I remember as though it were only yesterday. My twentieth birthday had come three weeks before, and after a very small celebration with honey cakes and dried figs—my family had tried to make the day cheerful—I went into my corner to my pile of rags and quietly cried myself to sleep.

You must understand, I had never seen sunlight or moonlight or starlight or lamplight. I had never seen the face of my mother or father or little sister. I had tried through my fingertips to capture some idea, but it was only a vague form, like the carved animals father had made for me as a boy.

No color was known to me—I had never seen the bright blue of the sky laced with white clouds; had never seen the orange-red of the poppies or the golden-yellows of the lilies, nor the green of spring grass nor the kaleidoscope crystal of the Kidron brook, nor the sparkling brown of my sister's eyes. I was blind—blind from the moment I came into the world. And a terrible despair had settled on me that I would leave the world in the same way—crying from eyes that would never see.

I had grown up in the blackness but was not aware that I was different until I was four. My parents protected me and patiently cared for me. Except for falling and continually running into things and being confined to our small courtyard, my little world was happy though strange.

Then slowly and in different ways, I began to realize that others did not have to feel their way around. They had something in their eyes that I did not have—something they called "sight"—which allowed them to feel things before they heard them or touched them. They could feel a sparrow without holding the quivering bunch of feathers in their hands; I could not. They could find the food on their plate without spilling it all over the cloth; I could not.

But I thought, perhaps I will. Perhaps someday I will open my eyelids, and sight—whatever wonder it is—will be there. I hoped and hoped, but gradually in my early teens realized I was doomed to blackness and to beggary. My little sister, Ruth, had brought this home to me. She was five years younger than I, and as a baby, was my delight. As she grew older, she left me in my darkness to play with other children, and I was terribly unhappy and lonely and angry. Then she visited the synagogue school and came home, telling me all about what they were doing. And she would take me on walks around the neighborhood and describe to me the potter working at his wheel, the tent-maker weaving the camel's hair, the carpenter shaping the wood with his draw knife. I realized that people worked, that boys grew to manhood and worked at some task, and I could not even learn to write like my little sister.

What does a blind man do? He begs. He sits in his darkness listening for steps. He holds up his bowl and he whines out his request for some charity. I would never work as a man, never know love or marry, never father a child of my own. I was just a shadow, something less than a human being. Oh, I tell you, my heart broke within me, and a bitterness and despair blacker than my blindness settled on me.

Daily Ruth took me stumbling to my begging place by the main road, leading north to the Temple area. Bless her, she tried so hard to find a place with a little shade, close enough, yet not so close that I might be stepped on by the passing camels and donkeys. She would bring my skimpy meal at noon and would try so hard to cheer me, telling me all the community gossip in her happy, piping voice; and I would try, for her sake, to seem happy myself. She was my brightest spot.

On Sabbath day, the family would take me to my place and then go on to the synagogue or occasionally the Temple. Sabbath day was the best day for begging, so I stopped going to the synagogue when I reached my eighteenth birthday; we needed the money, what little I brought in.

Synagogue worship had been enjoyable for me, but the Temple was forbidden to me since I was not whole. The chanting, the prayers, the reading of the Torah, the prophets; this was something I could do in part, so I memorized as much Scripture as I could, and as a child, prayed for a miracle.

It was Sabbath morning when it happened. I was sitting in my place, as usual, when I heard numerous sandaled feet approaching, voices murmuring, and smelled the ever-present dust of the street blowing past me. As the group came near, I grabbed my bowl and held it up and out—and then withdrew it in disgust and anger as the men began to discuss me as though I were an ox or a sheep.

"Who sinned, Lord? This fellow or his parents?"

"Neither this man sinned nor his parents," a very kind and thoughtful voice replied, "but in order that the works of God may be manifest in him. We must do the works of Him who sent me, as long as it is day; night is coming, when no man can work."

I could tell he was kneeling before me, could hear his quiet breathing, and then I felt his hand on my knee, and he quieted the fear that was beginning to rise in my mind with some strange and exciting words: "As long as I am in the world, I am the light of the World."

I heard him spit on the dusty ground, and a few seconds later he tenderly anointed my closed eyes with a thin layer of mud and told me to wash in the Pool of Siloam nearby.

He got up and walked away while I sat there like a dumb man. Out of the crowd that had gathered came one of my neighbors. He bent over me and asked if I wanted to go. Fear and hope wrestled in my heart. Would it fail to help and would I look like a fool? Ruth had told me of a man named Jesus who had worked miracles and preached about the Good News of God's kingdom. The men who had so coolly discussed me had called the kind-voiced man "Jesus."

"*That the works of God may be manifest in him,*" he had said. Could it be? I would go.

I knelt at the pool's edge, my heart beating like a drum, and very carefully washed off the clay. A strange sensation flashed through my eyes and head. I opened my eyes, and with a cry of pain, closed them again, throwing any hands over my face to shield my eyes from the dazzling light and that incredible miracle called "sight."

"I can see!" The thought raced over and over through my mind. As I cautiously opened my eyes once more, shading them with my hands, the words leaped to my mouth: "I can see! I can see!" Words cannot explain the joy and wonder that filled my mind.

I grabbed my startled neighbor and hugged him and then looked at his face, the first human face I had ever seen—there is nothing so warm as a human smile. And I cried so that tears, for a while, made everything hazy. Then, so excited I could hardly talk clearly, I said, "Show me the way home. I want to see Ruth, and I want to see my mother and father."

And we ran through the streets, laughing, shouting, and crying to my home. Along the way, people slowed us to ask what had happened. Neighbors came out and stared. "Is it really him? Is this Lemuel's blind son? Maybe he just looks like him."

The story was repeated, and soon a line of wondering people trailed us to my house.

I cannot describe for you the joy of my family and the funny way they kept coming back to me to ask again and again, "Can you really see? Am I not dreaming, my son?" Oh, how we praised God!

Well, it was decided by my family and neighbors that we should tell the rabbi immediately of such news, and I should see the Temple. Off we went, and I tried to take in everything along the way, looking and asking questions about all the new sights. The Temple was magnificent; I looked until my eyes hurt, and Ruth answered my continual barrage of questions.

The Pharisees were something else, though. I expected them to rejoice with me and to call on this Jesus to speak to us all. Instead, they were coldly skeptical and suspicious. They asked questions, and I told my story, and they began to argue among themselves, saying silly, insulting things about Jesus. Suddenly the leader stopped them and turned to me with a question: "What do you say about him, since he opened your eyes?"

My mind raced for an explanation. How did I really feel about him, this man who had given me a brand-new life? Out of my confusion came the words of Isaiah, "He hath sent me to proclaim release to the captives and recovering of sight to the blind." I blurted out, "He is a prophet."

This seemed to make the Pharisees and priests angry. They did not want to believe me, so they called for my parents. "Is this your son, who you say was born blind? Then how does he now see?"

I felt the fear in my parents' voices. Ruth had said that the Pharisees hated Jesus, and any of his followers would be thrown out of their synagogue. Mother and father loved the synagogue, and they loved me. They really did not know Jesus anyway. I should answer for myself.

They called me to the front of the crowd once more. Now I was getting angry. They were acting like stupid fools. Why did they have it in for such a kind wonder-working man like Jesus? They said, "Give God the praise; we know that this man is a sinner."

I said, "Whether he is a sinner or not, I do not know: one thing I know for certain, that once I was blind but now I can see."

Again they questioned: "What did he do to you? How did he open your eyes?"

My temper got the best of me. "I have told you already, but you do not listen. Why do you want to hear it again? Do you also want to be his disciples?"

Now they lost their tempers and called me some choice names. "You're the one who is his disciple. We are disciples of Moses. We know that God spoke to Moses; but this man—we don't even know where he came from."

I had recovered a little. "Now here's the extraordinary thing. You don't know where he came from, and yet he gave me the gift of sight. Everybody knows that God does not listen to sinners. It is the man who has proper respect for God and does what God wants him to do—he's the one God listens to."

By now they were turning purple with rage and getting ready to scream. I said, "Why, since the world began nobody's ever heard of a man who was born blind being given his sight. If this man did not come from God, he couldn't do such a thing."

"You misbegotten wretch. Are you trying to teach us? You are anathema."

One of the Temple guards gave me a shove that sent me falling into the crowd. The Pharisees yelled all sorts of insults at me, and my family and I left the Temple courts never to return. What a disappointment!

I felt terrible and for a couple of hours simply wandered around trying to think. Why did the leaders hate Jesus so? What was wrong with them? Then I sat on the Temple steps in the shade while my mind worked. I was so happy about my gift and all the possibilities it opened for me, and they had stolen the gladness from me. I just did not understand.

As I was sorting out my thoughts, I began to pray. I realized now that you could have sight and still be blind. You could have life and still not live. You could be religious and not really know God. I wanted to learn how a man could please God and be healed of his spiritual blindness. The Pharisees were right. I was a sinner, still just a beggar with a blind heart.

My old habits were strong, and I heard the steps before I looked up with my new eyes and I remembered the voice that had shattered the darkness. Jesus was looking for me.

We talked for a while—or I should say, I talked. I thanked him for the gift of sight and poured out all the turmoil in my heart. With great concern and compassion, he listened. Finally, he looked intently into my new eyes and asked me a question: "Do you believe in the Son of God?"

I replied, "Who is he, Sir, that I may believe, may commit myself to him?" And my heart trembled with anticipation that He might be the promised One of God.

"You have been seeing him."

Oh, I knew it, I knew it! And I fell at his feet, saying from my soul, "Lord, I believe. I give myself to you. I will be your servant."

And that's my story. How is it with you?

The Baby King

Matthew 2:1–16, 27:54; Luke 7:1–10

Listen, you know what's always fascinated me? Do you? Well, let me tell you. I've always been fascinated by the religious fantasies of Jews. You know, they have all kinds of quaint stories from their days of glory, long ago now. But there are also new things going on all the time for them. Did you know that?

Startling things. Some of them I've been in on myself.

Yes, I believe I *will* have another cup—just a small one. Helps you sleep better, you know.

By the way, my name is Quirinius. I'm assistant commander of the tower here in Jerusalem. Thirty-five years now I've been in the Emperor's service. I'll probably retire soon—somewhere like Philippi—maybe next year. I come from a military family, but I've got real good lineage on my mother's side. She was a daughter of Senator Cassius. Yeah, she's dead now. My father died of wounds received in Megiddo in a skirmish with those crazy zealots led by Theudas.

That reminds me: Let me finish telling you about these superstitious Jews. My first real encounter with their strange ways came right after I completed my training in Rome. I was assigned here in Jerusalem. I got here just in time to be given peacekeeping duties at a little village seven miles south of here.

Yep, Bethlehem, that's the place. Some town. The worst food and poorest accommodations I ever saw. Anyway, this big tax enrollment had been ordered by old Augustus, and people began pouring into this little town till it filled up and then some.

Nah, we didn't have much trouble—a few drunks, a few fights, mostly over gambling. But the last night we were there, this couple came in from up north.

They were just peasants, but this girl was about to have her baby. Imagine, they came all the way from someplace in Galilee. The inn was packed, so they made do in the stable. Anyway, peculiar things began that night.

For one thing, there was an unearthly stillness that sort of settled down over the whole town long about midnight. Kind of gave you the creeps. I guess the baby must have been born during that time. Anyway, when we made rounds at the third watch, I looked in on the couple, and everything was okay. The baby was sleeping in a feed trough. He looked like all babies, wrinkled and red. They already had swaddling bands on him. The man looked like he was gonna faint, but that young wife of his was real chipper, though mighty tired. The innkeeper's wife and a servant girl had helped with the birth. They were lucky they made it to Bethlehem in time. That baby could have come while they were still on the road.

Anyway, later that morning we had this bunch of shepherds from out on the hills come tromping into town. Guess what they were looking for. Yeah, for a new baby in a manger. Now that was what struck me. "How did they know?" I said to myself.

They came up with this terrific story about an angel—that's some kind of a heavenly spirit, I think—anyway, they claimed this shining angel had given them the word. Their God was giving them a Savior, Messiah, the Lord. Man, they were excited. They thought it was great. Claimed a whole chorus of these angel things were singing about it in the sky above the hills out there. Did you ever hear anything like that? It really sounded good: "Peace on earth, goodwill to men."

Peace, ha! The poor fools didn't know it, but we were planning a new invasion of Africa that spring. Not much peace except where the legions rule, you know. "Pax Romana."

I'm not drunk—pour me a little more. Thanks, that's right good wine.

You know, the gods never did anything for me. No breaks. And I've really tried hard.

Well, where was I? Oh yeah. I went with the shepherds—they were a smelly bunch—to the inn stable. Know what those fellas did? Got down on their knees and bowed their heads to the ground, kinda whispering in Hebrew the whole time: *"Hallel Adonai, Yeshua, Messiah!"* They had tears in their eyes, mind you—that rough bunch of clods. They really meant it. They even left some of their precious lambs as gifts for the baby. He was named Jesus.

Must have been about fourth watch in the morning by then, and guess what those crazy shepherds did. They went around waking up their families and friends, and next thing you know the whole town is going around *"kadoshing"* God. That word *"kadosh"* means "glory." I've picked up a lot of Hebrew myself.

What do you mean? No, I'm not done. What's the matter, ain't I a good customer? Pour!

Well, that afternoon we moved back to Jerusalem, and I forgot all about it. Then about five months later, these funny-looking strangers came riding into the big city and scared old Herod silly. Turned out they were some kind of minor kings from Persia, or maybe it was Armenia. Anyway, now get this—these characters were looking for a special baby too, a Jewish king, a savior. How about that?

Remember that baby's name? Jesus. In Hebrew, that's *Yeshua*, "savior."

Herod really got excited. He called in all the priests and astrologers and rabbis, the whole works, and demanded to know all about it and why he hadn't been informed and all that. He was a shrewd one. After he calmed down, he told the wisemen to please find the baby and come back and tell him so he could pay it proper homage.

For some reason, they never came back, and Herod got so mad and frightened it was unbelievable. Course he did something about it—he decided to kill all the male children in Bethlehem who were two years old and younger. I know. I was in charge of the detail that had to do the killing. It still makes me sick to think about it. It's no wonder that the Jews hate us. I still have nightmares after thirty years.

But you know what? We didn't find that baby king. I'm sure that baby born in the stable was really the one Herod wanted destroyed—but he was gone. No one even knew where his parents had gone. Now, is that strange or isn't it?

No, I'm not finished, blast it! Get me another cup or I'll break your head!

The real corker to this whole thing is coming up. Yeah, the baby king grew up. I'm sure it's him. They call him Jesus, the Savior, and they say he's a great teacher—a miracle worker, a Messiah. Now I'm not sure he was born in Bethlehem, but everything else fits. He's just about the age that baby would be now, and the same mysterious things are going on again. You ought to see the crowds that follow him around. You wouldn't believe some of the things he has done.

I have a friend, a centurion like me—in fact, we were in training together in Rome. Anyway, he is stationed up at Capernaum. He has gone sort of overboard on this Jewish religion bit. The truth is, he even built one of those synagogues where the Jews worship, and he might have done some worshipping himself. But about two years ago he had a servant who was in bad shape, on the point of dying as I recall. Crispus was frantic about this old servant; I think the man had been with him ever since he'd been commissioned. Crispus was always too tender-hearted. I remember how much trouble he had when we did our combat practice—but he's a good soldier. Anyway, this Jesus came through Capernaum and healed that servant, saved his life—without even going near the man. Crispus swears it's so.

Now I'm gonna let you in on a little secret. The Jewish leaders had Jesus arrested tonight. He has really given them a hard time. Only this time, he won't get away, my friend. They're out for blood and they know how to work Pilate.

Know who'll have to do the crucifixion—probably tomorrow? Yeah, me. That's right, me. I'll be in charge of the detail. Looks like we're gonna find out if he really is a Messiah or just another phony.

Listen, you know what I'm gonna do? I've got it all figured out. I'll have some time alone with him while we get ready to flog him. Guess what I'm gonna say to him. I'm gonna ask him, "Jesus, were you born in Bethlehem? Are you that baby king from the stable? The one the wisemen were looking for?"

Yeah. I'm going to ask him, "Are you the one they've been waiting for?"

[Pause]

Yes, I'm back. It's been a rough day. Just fill my cup. I've never seen anyone die like he did. I believe he really was God's special Son!

The Man Who Took My Place

Matthew 27:15–26

No problem. You want to know how I feel so you can go and make a report for King Herod's court? Am I supposed to be this evening's entertainment? Ha. Well, for the right price, I'll tell you.

How do I feel? I feel great. Fantastic!

Sometimes a panic kind of grabs me—like what if I'm dreaming and it's not for real? What if I wake up suddenly and I'm back in that stinking cell, hungry, filthy, waiting to be flogged and hung, waiting to die? That scares me—makes it hard to go to sleep, you know? But, hey, a cup or two of wine, and I'll drop right off. The nightmares are bound to stop—someday.

I mean, I actually watched the crucifixion take place, all the time thinking, "That was supposed to be me!"

I had to see who this fellow was who was hated more than they hated me.

Politicians—I don't understand them, but I'm grateful this time. What a weird bunch: Sadducees, Pharisees, Pilate, and even the Herodians ganging up on a country carpenter. Some show. Jesus must have really riled them to have been put in my place.

I have no idea what that Jesus did that made them hate him so much. The prison grapevine was full of all kinds of talk. Most of the rumors had it that he was a religious fanatic of some sort, another Messiah type. Stories of miracles—healings of all kinds, a blind man here in town, and get this, a dead man was supposedly raised to life out at Bethany. How about that? I understand that was the shocker that made the Sanhedrin get down to serious business.

But what I don't understand is why they would get so excited about a religious fanatic, even one who did miracles. It's not like there haven't been plenty of these guys popping up all over the place over the years. Except all the others didn't amount to anything compared to this Galilean. This fellow was teaching things that could destroy the way things work around here. He seemed to ignore the Law and traditions. He declared the hope of forgiveness for all men, not just Jews, and insisted that God loved all men regardless. Now you know that can't be true!

During the months I rotted in that cell, I gave a lot of thought to some of the strange things Jesus was supposed to be teaching. The Pharisees claimed that he thought he was God's Son in some bizarre way. How could that be? They had to get rid of him.

I know, given what I've done and where I've ended up, I don't seem like the kind of man who would be interested in this kind of stuff, but I'll tell you: there was a time—long ago—when I dreamed of being a rabbi. Now my life's a total mess, but I still hope, my friend. And I still hate Rome.

But that Jesus fellow. I'm still not sure what to make of him. I had pretty well written him off until yesterday as just another crazy. But that was before I watched him die. It was eerie, all that went on. Mind you, I've seen quite a few executions, but never one like this. Never!

One of my friends died out there with him, you know. Good ol' Demas. I hated to see him go like that—better a dagger thrust under the ribcage than that blasted torture on the cross. You see, it began to get dark after they hung them. Then it thundered something awful, and sometimes the ground rolled like the thunder. Scared a lot of curious folks away—superstitious, I guess. I stayed on and watched and listened. Strange—the whole business!

The first thing he did was completely out of line: he prayed. Now I've heard lots of guys pray when they were dying or thought they were. Heard some of 'em curse and scream their heads off, too. You can't pray when you're being flogged, except inside—you don't have enough breath to do anything but hurt.

But Jesus started praying, quiet-like, I think, while they were putting in the spikes. What got me—he wasn't praying for himself, but for the ones who were crucifying him. And not only for the soldiers, but for the Pharisees and the scribes and priests—for everybody, maybe even me. He prayed over and over to some God he called *Abba*, "father." Doesn't that beat anything you ever heard of? Imagine thinking of God as your own father!

After a couple of hours of yelling insults, the priests and Pharisees left. They really let him have it: "Since you are the Son of God, come down from that cross and we'll all follow you. If you can destroy the Temple and rebuild it in three days, surely you can jump off that cross! You saved others; why don't you do a little saving of yourself?" They got tired finally and left.

One young man moved up closer with a couple of older women, weeping. Jesus said something to that man about "your mother" and the man nodded while the older woman cried harder. I expect it was Jesus's mother and some friends. In a little while they slipped back with some others huddled nearby.

More time passed and he seemed to be praying again. All at once he said something loudly in Hebrew, like he was pleading with someone close by. My Hebrew's pretty rusty, so I didn't get it all—there were some words about being left, forsaken by God. His face looked terribly anxious about whatever it was. I thought he was crying.

Just after noon, the sky got darker than I've ever seen it, with a greenish cast reflected in the lightening. It was scary. Even the soldiers, tough as they are, talked about leaving for shelter. Thought about it myself.

Then another strange thing happened. My friend, Demas, got into a yelling match with the other crook who was up there being executed, arguing about who deserved what, fearing God, and why Jesus wasn't helping them escape. Lo and behold, Jesus responded by promising my friend that they would be together in a place called Paradise—that very day. Can you imagine anything more ridiculous than that? There they are, dying in agony, and Demas says: "Lord Jesus, remember me when you come into your kingdom."

And Jesus said to Demas: "Truly I tell you, today with me you shall be in Paradise." After that, a peace came over my friend's face and he smiled at me with his swollen lips—I could swear he did.

They must have been hanging there for five or six hours, eyes closed, barely able to breathe, hurting all over, begging for water— Jesus did too, as I recall. They offered him some of that drugged wine; and he just shook his head. The bleeding had stopped but the sweat poured. Flies were all over them—awful, sickening, trying to die, I guess.

Then all at once Jesus opened his eyes like he saw someone. With agonizing effort he yelled as loudly as he could, "*Tetelesthai*," which means, "It's all finished."

You have to wonder what he meant by that. Was he just giving up, or had he completed something he wanted to do?

One of the guards who knows me from having put me in the drunk tank several dozen times was especially impressed. He says that Jesus deliberately died just a little bit before sunset. Get this: before Jesus stopped breathing, he prayed again to his *Abba* God, "Father, into your hands I commit my spirit." He could barely whisper it.

Then he bowed his head and died, in half the time it usually takes. How do you account for that?

I'm not sure what I think about Jesus now. What if he's right about that stuff he's been teaching? What if he's right about God? He surely believed it.

One thing I do know: I'll never forget the man who took my place.

Would you?

Interview with the Governor

John 18:28–19:22

[To Reporter/Audience:] Good morning. Yes, thank you. Welcome. Yes, I am Pontius Pilate. Please have a seat.

Of course. Think nothing of it. As governor, I'm always happy to speak with The Roman Tribune and share anything your readers might consider to be of interest.

When did I first meet Jesus from Galilee? Do you really want to talk about him?

Oh, well, all right. Our first meeting took place early Friday morning, very early in fact—when the Jewish leaders of our city brought him to me with a demand for his death. He had supposedly done something that violated their religious Laws. This sort of thing is always happening. And they are always squabbling among themselves—a lot of jealousy and bickering, jockeying for position and whatnot.

Of course, I had heard of him before. Rumors fly around this old city like pigeons, you know. I've heard all kinds of tales about miracles—healing of blind people, lame people, various sicknesses, leprosy cures—mind you, even a resuscitation over at Bethany not long ago. Pretty weird stuff, really.

Actually, he was just a peasant from up north—from Nazareth, I believe. His real problem was that he talked a little too much. He was preaching and teaching all over, and he tangled with both the Pharisees and the Sadducees. Didn't know when to stop. When he began to be a threat to their positions, that was it. A typical would-be Messiah. The Jews have had a hundred in the last fifty years. They start little rebellions but don't amount to much.

Do I believe he was really guilty?

He may have been, but remember I was acting basically on the charges that Caiaphas and the Sanhedrin brought against him. They lined up some witnesses who couldn't even get their stories straight. But the main charge was claiming to be their Messiah, something about being the Son of their God. This amounted to blasphemy according to them, and by their sacred Law, he deserved to die.

Adding to this was his strange behavior. The man simply would not defend himself. He was silent throughout most of my examination. He talked about his kingship, and that cleared up one of their charges, incidentally. Said he was a king, was indeed born to it, but his kingdom was spiritual and his followers would not bear arms on his behalf. He said he came into the world to bear witness to the truth. Everyone who was looking for the truth would listen to him. I recall I asked, "What is truth?"

He didn't respond, just looked at me. After that, he said practically nothing.

What's that? Didn't I try to release him?

Well, yes, you could say that. You see, the Jews have a very special holy day at this time of the year. They butcher lambs and observe a feast called the Passover. Goes way back in their history. We have tried to add a little to the festivities by releasing a Jewish prisoner during the feast, usually a political criminal. This Jesus was innocent in my thinking, and I tried to make a deal with the crowd. I offered to release Jesus or Barabbas, thinking Jesus would be chosen. Barabbas, you see, was a lousy character, suspected of several robberies and a proven murderer.

But you wouldn't believe it; they screamed for me to release Barabbas and crucify Jesus. We nearly had a riot. Dreadful thing, quite disturbing. I detest mob violence.

One word from Jesus would have helped. You know, he is absolutely the strangest prisoner I've ever had. He would not talk—I think I mentioned that—until I said, "Don't you realize that I have the power of life or death over you?" I thought the poor man would break and fall on his knees and beg for mercy. Not him. I could swear a smile crossed his lips, and guess what he said, calm as you please—as if I were *his* prisoner: "You have no power over me at all except that which has been granted you from above." Now what do you think of that?

My wife? You want to hear about the note from my wife? Really? Word gets around, doesn't it?

Well, you know how it is sometimes. My wife has had a religious thing going for years, always trying out new cults. When she heard about this fellow Jesus, she went to hear him teach over at the Temple a couple of times. She was really concerned about his death, and I guess she had a nightmare or something. She did write a note asking me to forget the whole thing. But I couldn't do that. I'd have been laughed out of the palace if word got around that my wife was running the show here. Come to think of it, she's still a little upset.

What's that? Did I yield to political pressure by delivering Jesus to the Jews?

I suppose you could put it that way. You have to understand that a man in my position must protect his interests and maintain Rome's peace and order. The empire must come first, you know.

You have to recall that he was accused of some rather damaging, even dangerous charges. There was this business about being a king and forbidding tribute to our glorious Caesar, as well as causing trouble among the important Jews. When the high priest and his bunch want somebody dead as badly as they wanted Jesus dead, there must be real trouble. I acted as Caesar's friend and maintained the people's goodwill.

How do I *feel* about it?

My friend, it's over and done with. I do not let this sort of thing bother me. I have no regrets. I was merely doing my duty. I refuse to be held responsible for simply carrying out orders. Haven't you been told how I handled that? After pleading with the Jews and the mob to change their minds—remember, there was about to be a riot—I delivered Jesus to them. But not until I had called for a basin of water. My servant held it up where everyone could see, and I washed my hands of the whole affair. "I am innocent of this righteous man's blood," I said. "See to it yourselves."

Their reply was positively chilling. They said, "His blood will be on us and our children." They know who's at fault.

Rumors of resurrection? His promise to rise from the dead and resume leading his followers?

Well. That's nothing more than religious imagination. You know how these religious fanatics are. I'm not superstitious. They checked him while he still on the cross, and believe me, he was dead. A spear thrust in the vitals proved that, if you know what I mean.

This will probably finish this whole would-be Christ thing and his following.

They will doubtless dwindle and fade away in the next few months. After all, a dead Messiah . . .

Excuse me. Excuse me just a moment.

[To Centurion:] Centurion, get a hold of yourself! I can't understand a word you say when you speak so quickly. What? What's that? The guards say what?

Who has been seen alive? How is that even possible?

What are you telling me? They claim to have seen angels? Angels! This cannot be. This can't be true. Jesus from Galilee is alive?

Have you lost your mind?

[To Reporter/Audience:] Do you believe what you are hearing?

Escape to Freedom

The Book of Philemon

Early in the morning—very early in the morning, while the moon hung like a silver fingernail on the western horizon—I began my escape to freedom.

I had been born into slavery. My father and mother were slaves. They both had awfully rough lives. From what my mother told me, my father came into slavery as a baby in his mother's arms. As Syrian peasants fought the Romans many years ago, the village was overrun, and they were captured and sold.

My mother had been twelve years old when Arab traders bought her in Damascus. She was an orphan. The Arabs got a good price for her from a merchant in Laodicea, who resold her to the family in Colosse. My father was chief steward of the household when she came. About a year later, they became husband and wife—as much as slaves ever can, at least.

I think they really loved each other, and they got along beautifully except for one thing. My father had a fierce desire to be free and was rather outspoken about it. Mother thought it dangerous, since such talk could be considered insurrection.

When I came along, they gave me a typical slave name, Useful. They were optimistic, I guess. The master of the house did not interfere with their relationship, which gave me an unexpected bit of security and a real father. Make no mistake—when I was a child, I was responsible for numerous chores and had to steal time for playing. The best job was tending the horses. They were my friends and playmates, and I was able to spend hours roaming the pastures, almost free. I learned to ride bareback by the time I was six, mounting from a fence or a tree. That turned out to be preparation for my escape to freedom.

Shortly after my sixteenth birthday, my father was killed by a field slave who went crazy on opium. It was grown near our place, and many slaves used it. This man went berserk. He had been using a knife to skin some butchered goats, and when my father criticized the sloppy job he was doing, he began screaming and crying. My father turned to go and get another man to help, and the crazy one stabbed him in the back. I thought for a while my mother would die too—just from her grief.

Our master hired another steward, a Greek, much older, very fat, and extremely lazy. I hated the new steward because he put so much of his work off on the rest of us, something my father never did. The only good thing about him was his storytelling. He had been everywhere and seen everything, and he could almost make you see it too. Corinth, Ephesus, Rome—they would come alive as he told his tales.

Six years after my father's death, my mother died of small pox and I was left alone. My father's ambition, plus the Greek's stories of far-off places, set me to thinking about running away. I wanted to be my own boss, to be free. If I could get far enough away, I might be able to make it as a free man. I had never been marked or branded, so I had a chance. I could take one of the horses and ride to Laodicea, and then to Miletus, and with any luck at all, find a ship going to Corinth or maybe even to Rome.

Money was my biggest problem. Selling the horse in Miletus wouldn't provide enough for the ship's passage. I had to have more. There was just one place to get it. On the evening before market day, our owner would give, as usual, a large sum of money to the old Greek so that he could start for the market early on Thursday. I could slip into his room easily enough, get the money, slip out to the stable for a horse, and be gone before anyone had the least suspicion.

My plan worked beautifully. Not even the horses betrayed me. After all, they had known me for years.

I decided to avoid Laodicea, lest I be recognized. Cutting west across country, I hit the main road for Miletus and the harbor. A little over a hundred miles would see me safely aboard a ship bound for somewhere—a free man.

I took it easy, planning to travel until daylight and then find cover. Just before dawn, I spotted a grove of trees with a small stream running through it. A perfect place. The horse grazed, and I slept until noon.

I got out some dried fruit from my small bag of provisions and happily chewed while I watched the traffic on the road from my hiding place. It was great to be free.

As soon as it was dark, I mounted and rode on. At one point, I was frightened out of my wits by a cohort of Roman cavalry that came riding out of the darkness behind me, cursing and laughing, their armor clattering. Their noise warned me just in time, and I slipped off the road and into some brush until they passed. I was holding my breath, afraid my horse might whinny or shy and give me away.

Further down the road, I saw that the soldiers had stopped at a crossroads tavern for the night. All the horses were tethered outside, and a stable boy stood uneasy watch. I carefully walked my horse a safe distance around the tavern and kept going.

The next day and night were uneventful except that I was running out of food. The third night, at about the fourth watch, I reached the outskirts of Miletus. I was so excited I almost forgot my hunger pains. I waited just outside the city walls until daylight and then rode in with a group of farmers, carrying ducks, chickens, and geese for sale in the market.

I was so hungry by then that I decided to wait until after breakfast to sell the horse. I went to a tavern and ordered a meal. The serving girl was friendly, so I asked her where I might sell my horse. She said she didn't know but would ask her master. A big burly, man with a greasy beard walked to my table and looked me over coldly.

"So you have a horse to sell, eh? Did you steal it? You couldn't be a runaway, could you?"

I realized then that my clothes were not those of a man who could afford to ride a horse. And with a sinking feeling in my stomach, I knew too that he would question why I had no saddle. It was a dead giveaway. How could I have been so stupid? But I didn't give up yet.

I protested his questions and challenged him to find any slave mark on me.

All at once he smiled and said, "Relax, finish your meal. I'll buy your horse myself." He smiled again and went to the kitchen.

I thought that I had it made then, and I finished my breakfast with zest, including some second helpings. As the girl cleared the dishes, the big man came over and sat down. He took out his purse. "I'll give you ten denarii for your horse. I've looked him over already."

"But he's worth double that," I heard myself say.

The tavern owner just smiled again. "You'll take ten and be glad, or I'll call the guard here so quickly your head will swim. Mark or no mark, you're a slave. You don't fool me. I've seen hundreds just like you. Here's your money, now get gone."

I was really in trouble. He could turn me in for a reward if he decided to, so I grabbed the coins and left.

As I started up the street, the serving girl grabbed me and pulled me back into the alley.

"Listen," she said, "he's going to call the guard and claim you stole the money from him. Then he'll have your horse, your money, and a reward for catching a runaway. He does it all the time."

Fear seemed to paralyze me. I felt like the world was caving in on me. What could I do? What could I possibly do?

"Hide!" said the girl.

"Where? They'll find me easily in this town."

"Hide where they won't look—on the roof of the tavern. Wait until you see my master leave, then slip back in, and I'll show you where to go. No one is around this time of day. Tonight, you can go to the harbor and take passage on a boat. One leaves for Rome in the morning, the sailors say."

"Can you get me some other clothes? I'm a marked man in these."

"Maybe, when I go to the market."

"Here's a denarius. Or do you want more to keep quiet?"

"Oh, no," she frowned. "I'm not doing this for money," she said indignantly. "I hate my master, and I like you, that's all."

"Thank you. I owe you my life." I knew I had to trust her; there wasn't any other way.

"I must get back now," she said. "Watch for my master to leave, and then come on in. They won't look for you here."

I did exactly as she said, and somehow, I made it out of Miletus. In the clothes she found for me to wear, I had no trouble boarding the grain ship for Rome, although it took nearly all my money. I'll never forget the unexpected help I found at the Anchor Tavern in Miletus.

The trip to Rome was exciting and fun except for two days of seasickness and the fact that I was broke when we landed at the harbor that served Rome, the great Eternal City set on seven hills. The city is so huge and so crowded and so cruel, it's unbelievable. People died in the streets from disease and hunger and mayhem every night. I couldn't beg a crumb of food anywhere in the wharf area and had my life threatened several times for just asking. So I started walking toward Rome proper, wondering what it would be like to starve to death.

By nightfall, I was still five miles from the city, hungrier than I had ever been in my life, exhausted, and ready to give it all up. I saw a light a little way off the cobblestone highway and tried to get my tired legs to carry me there. Maybe they could spare a little water at least.

At first, I thought I was delirious. I heard singing like I'd never heard before, full of joy and cheer. A strange sight lay before me. A group of slaves sat around a fire eating, talking, and often breaking into song as though they were celebrating. I stumbled into their circle ready to beg or be beaten—and they welcomed me as if they knew me. Warm food was placed in my hands as soon as I sat down, and another man handed me a cup of watered wine. They urged me to eat first— slowly—and talk later. I did.

Then they talked. Oh, what stories they could tell! But you had to believe them. They were a bunch of slaves on their way to the harbor without even so much as an overseer or chief steward to watch them. They carried money to get a load of goods for their wealthy master.

"How can your owner trust you? Why don't you run like me? How does he know you won't cheat him?"

The same simple answer was given to all my questions: "He is a Christian, and so are we. He treats us like brothers, and the Lord expects us to behave."

I couldn't believe it. As the fire died, they prayed to their God asking him to help me, Useful, for Jesus's sake. I wondered who this Jesus, so important to them, could be.

I slept through the night like one dead, until I was gently awakened. They shared their simple breakfast and gave me an address in Rome where I would be received as a friend. Again they prayed, and we parted company.

A little before noon, I arrived in Rome. The city awed me and pleased me. It was immense and very beautiful in parts. It was also dirty and full of beggars, crowded with people and animals going in a hundred different directions. I asked for help from several Romans and was turned away. Finally a woman helped me, and after a couple of mistakes and more directions, I found myself before the door of a plain, almost poor home not far from the Imperial Palace.

I knocked and the door opened, revealing a very kind-looking man probably in his early sixties. He invited me in. I explained how I came there, and he smiled at my perplexing questions.

"Before I answer any questions," he said to me, "there are others to meet and a meal to eat. Please come with me."

He led me into a shady courtyard. There, under a tree, sitting at a table being prepared by several servants, was a slightly built, slightly balding Jew.

Sitting next to him was a Roman soldier, which startled me, as you can well imagine. The soldier and the little old Jew were chained together. Two other men sat at the table, one a Greek, the other a Syrian like myself.

The Jew was dictating a letter while the Greek wrote and everyone else listened intently, including the soldier. My guide, Luke, for such was his name, introduced me to the Apostle Paul, to Epaphras, to Demas, and to the two "servants," who were only acting as servants, John Mark and Aristarchus. They were to become my dearest friends. Paul became my father in the Lord.

I stayed at the house five months, until the weather was right for sailing again. Paul introduced me to Jesus Christ, who became my Savior and my Master. As we talked and Paul taught through the long winter evenings, it became clear to me that I must return to my master, Philemon. I knew he was a kind man but had never questioned his religious persuasion, though my father and mother had often discussed his strange God. Now I realized Philemon was a Christian and I had done him a grave injustice.

Restitution must be made.

But it was no easy decision. Freedom is a precious condition, which you do not easily lay aside. But I had a new freedom now, the freedom to do right and be right, and I had to express it.

It's early in the morning and the moon once again is a silver crescent on the western horizon. In an hour or so I shall be home again. I have a letter from the Apostle to my master.

I'm not really sure how Philemon will respond—but I know there is a new Onesimus, a new "Useful," coming home to serve. I've been given so much!

You make a mess of your life, and God carefully arranges for you to have a new one. Useful finally and genuinely becomes "useful."

You run up a debt you cannot pay, and another pays it for you, because he cares. One friend on a cross, the other in a personal note.

You fill your life with fear, resentment, and frustration, and Jesus gives you his love and his presence and his power.

You long for freedom to do as you please, looking for happiness, and God makes you free in the midst of your bondage, free to please him, giving you a happiness beyond circumstances, and a wholeness of spirit.

You feel all alone with no place to really call home, and the Lord gives you his family and his Father's house forever.

O praise his name, I've escaped to freedom. Would you go with me?

Are you running this hour, caught up in a slavery of your own selfishness and sinning? Let him set you free.

Are you afraid and angry and frustrated with an enormous debt you can never repay? Let him love you and pay it for you.

Acquitted As Guilty

Romans 3:19–26; Isaiah 53:4–6

The vast arena lined with faces was the first thing I remember. It was a sort of huge municipal stadium filled with people—people who were connected with me in one way or another, I soon realized.

Then I saw this strange courtroom in the center of the arena. My jailor called it "the judgment seat." My bailiff, Pneuma, called it "the mercy seat." It was magnificently built from unusual stone that shone—a soft, white light glowed in the stone itself.

Something was missing, though. There was the judge's bench, the recorder's desk, the witness stand, but no jury box.

My escort led me up the first steps, and my excitement turned to dread. My footsteps made no sound on the strange surface, and the whole stadium was quiet now, waiting. Fear welled up within me. I trembled. My palms became clammy, and my stomach tied into knots. We marched up the last of the marble-like steps and down the long aisle.

A man appeared—at least he looked like a man—and gestured and asked in a loud voice, "Shall not the Judge of all the earth do right?"

The crowd in the arena fell to its knees with one motion, one sound, and every head bowed and every voice said, "Amen!"

I did likewise.

The Judge entered. There was an intense light, and within it, the shadowy figure of a person. The recorder entered and said to me, "Arise and face the bench."

I could hardly stand, but my comforter helped me. Now I noticed a gleaming inscription carved into the Judge's bench: "Truly, truly, I say unto you, except your righteousness shall exceed the righteousness of the scribes and Pharisees, ye shall in no wise enter into the kingdom of heaven."

A terrible lump came up in my throat. The recorder spoke again, "This is the case of Frank Brown, your Majesty."

I thought to myself, So it is for my sake that we are assembled.

The Judge answered in a quiet voice full of massive restraint, "How many witnesses against the defendant are there?"

The recorder's answer I could hardly believe: "Six hundred and twenty-three primary witnesses, my Lord."

The recorder began to call their names, and they appeared, one by one. I recognized many of them, but not all were familiar. My wife, my children, my mother and my father, my brother and sister, my uncles and aunts, my grandparents, my cousins, my schoolmates, my teachers, my employers, my sergeant and platoon leader, my roommate at college, the postman, paperboy—they passed by without looking at me. They stopped before the Judge, and each one related an incident—how I had lied, of petty theft, cheating, cruelty, lust, contempt, gossip, hatred, lack of respect, stubborn pride, greed, injustice, selfishness, ingratitude, dishonesty, misuse of body and talents.

When all 623 had finished, the recorder said, "There is, beside all this, the record of his thoughts and secret deeds, and all the good he failed to do."

The Judge spoke quietly: "It is enough." I thought to myself, I am doomed.

Then as judgment was to be pronounced, a man stepped from behind the bench and walked to my side. There was a radiance in his face, and scars could be seen on his hands. The great voice was unleashed now, and in overpowering tones, the Judge addressed the entire assembly: "I declare Frank Brown not guilty and free from all charges brought in this court."

The vast stadium responded, "Amen. Worthy is the Lamb."

Everything began to swim before my eyes, and I must have lost consciousness. As sight returned, I found myself sitting on a bench in the midst of a fog. Pneuma sat beside me, my comforter. "How can it be?" I heard myself asking. "How can I possibly be acquitted when I was so obviously guilty and deserving of everlasting punishment? If he is the Judge of all the earth and does right, he cannot free me. It is an awful mistake, and in a moment I'll be back in court."

Pneuma said, "No, Frank, the Judge made no mistake. Consider how he's treated you the past few years. Think how many great and wondrous blessings have been yours. Think of the peace, the joy, the purpose, the love that has reached into every relationship—in short, the new life that is yours, Frank."

"You're right, of course, but I don't see how he can do it!"

"My friend, the answer is where all the answers are," said Pneuma. He reached into my shirt pocket and pulled out the New Testament that had replaced my cigarettes. "Look, it is here, in Romans 3:19–26."

> "Now we know that, whatever the Law says, it speaks to those who are under the Law, that every mouth may be closed, and all the world may become accountable to God; because by the works of the Law no flesh will be justified in His sight; for through the Law comes the knowledge of sin. But now apart from the Law the righteousness of God has been manifested, being witnessed by the Law and the Prophets, even the righteousness of God through faith in Jesus Christ for all those who believe; for there is no distinction; for all have sinned and fall short of the glory of God being justified as a gift by His grace through the redemption which is in Christ Jesus; whom God displayed publicly as a propitiation in His blood through faith. This was to demonstrate His righteousness, because in the forbearance of God, He passed over the sins previously committed for the demonstration, I say, of His righteousness at the present time that He might be just and the justifier of the one who has faith in Jesus."

"But I'm afraid I still don't understand," I said.

Pneuma replied, "God declared you not guilty even though you were guilty, and he has treated you just as if you'd never sinned because of two events. Hold my hand," my comforter said, "and I'll show you."

As though in a dream, I found myself in a jostling crowd of dirty human beings, pushing and being pushed out through a huge, arched gateway in a thick, old wall made of tremendous stones. Snatches of conversation in a strange language left me just as puzzled as ever until we began to climb a winding hill. The procession was moving slowly, and I could see the reason up ahead. A group of Roman soldiers surrounded two men who were half carrying, half dragging huge wooden crosses. Another prisoner bowed beside the dark-skinned man who helped carry his cross, apparently too broken to do it alone. Oh, I knew now where I was and where we were going and who that tired figure tugging on his cross was. I cannot describe for you the next few hours. My eyes were too filled with tears and too ashamed to linger on the scene.

But the scripture flashed again and again in my mind: "God set Him forth a sacrifice on my behalf."

On my behalf and in my place. As it says in Isaiah 53:4–6:

> "Surely our griefs He Himself bore, And our sorrows He carried;
> Yet we ourselves esteemed Him stricken, Smitten of God, and afflicted.
> But He was pierced through for our transgressions, He was crushed for our iniquities;
> The chastening for our well-being fell upon Him, and by His scourging we are healed.
> All of us like sheep have gone astray, Each of us has turned to his own way;
> But the Lord has caused the iniquity of us all to fall on Him."

He bore my due, paid my debt, provided my ransom that the Judge might say: "I declare Frank Brown not guilty and free from all charges."

Oh, Praise His name! I could see it now. But Pneuma had said two events. I had seen only one. And as I realized this, darkness fell.

Suddenly I was awake in the darkness, there in my own bed, troubled, torn from sleep by my guilty, sinful heart. It had happened before, and in the quiet darkness with only the sound of my wife's gentle breathing beside me.

Pneuma spoke to me, "Frank, do you remember that Saturday night, five years ago, when you finally decided to stop running? Do you remember? You said, 'Okay, Lord, you've got me cornered. I'm so tired of my old sinful, selfish life, my sorriness, my failure to be a man, my temper, my inability to love, the way I keep hurting those I love. God, I'm sorry for the way I've treated you. I've fought you, resented you, insulted you, feared you, and run from you. Now, I'm giving up.'

"Do you remember that Sunday morning, Frank, how uneasy you were, how scared, how determined? You hardly listened to the sermon, Frank, and when the invitation came, with a smile and tears, you walked to your pastor, and the two of you talked with the Lord about your commitment.

"That's the other event, Frank, that made it possible," Pneuma explained. "The agonizing death of your Savior would have meant nothing unless you became willing to accept in trust what he had done for you and surrender yourself to him."

That judgment was, for me, the most unexpected mercy. Are you ready?

Glossary

Abba: Greek, "father" (Romans 8:15)

Abdon: Proper name (Judges 12:13)

Ahimilech: Proper name (1 Samuel 21:1ff)

Aristarchus: Proper name (Acts 19:29; Philemon 24; Colossians 4:10)

bar mitzvah: Aramaic, Hebrew, a ceremony for Jewish boys age thirteen and older who are deemed ready to participate in worship services; "*bar*" is Aramaic for "son," and "*mitzvah*" is Hebrew for "of the Law" (i.e., any of the group of 613 commandments or precepts present in or derived from the Old Testament)

Bethlehem Ephratah: Geographical description taken from Micah's prophecy distinguishing Bethlehem in Judah from Bethlehem in Galilee (Micah 5:2)

Capernaum: Major city in Galilee, the center of Jesus's ministry

Cassius: Roman, fictional name from Shakespeare's "Julius Caesar"

Colossae: City in Phrygia, Asia Minor, near Laodicea, location of early Christian church receiving Paul's Letter to the Colossians (Colossians 1:2)

Crispus: Latin, proper name (Acts 18:8)

Demas: Proper name (Philemon 24; Colossians 4:14)

denarius (plural, denarii): Latin, Roman silver coin, approximately
a day's wage (Matthew 18:28; Mark 6:37)

Elihu: Proper name (1 Samuel 1:1; Job 32:2,4,5)

Epaphras: Proper name (Philemon 23; Colossians 1:7)

Ephesus: City in Asia Minor (Acts 18:19,21; 1 Corinthians 15:32);
also one of the Seven Churches of Asia (Revelation 2:1)

Gadarene demoniac: Refers to Gadara in the Decapolis, where
Jesus healed a demon-possessed man (Matthew 8:28;
Mark 5:1)

Golgatha: Greek and Aramaic, the place where Jesus was cruci-
fied, which means "skull place" (Matthew 27:33; Mark
15:22; John 19:17)

Hallel Adonai: Hebrew, "Praise the Lord"

Herodians: Family and followers of King Herod of Galilee (30 BC
to 4 BC), and Herod Antipas of Galilee (4 BC to AD
39)

Hyrcanus: One of the Hasmonean rulers (63 BC to 40 BC) following the time of John II of the Maccabees

Jairus: Proper name (Mark 5:22, Luke 8:41)

Joash: Proper name, father of Gideon (Judges 6:11, 29–30)

kadosh: Hebrew, "praise" or "glorify"

kadoshim: Hebrew, "praising" or "glorifying"

kadoshing: Colloquialism for *kadoshim*

Kemuel: Proper name (Genesis 22:21)

Kidron: Valley and brook outside the walls of Jerusalem on the
eastern side of the city, near the Mount of Olives

Laodicea: City of Phrygia, near Colossae (Colossians 4:13t), one of
the Seven Churches of Asia (Revelation 3:14)

Lemuel: Proper name (Proverbs 31:1,4)

Machir: Proper name, son of Manasseh (Numbers 26:29, 32:40)

Megiddo: fortified city where the pass across Mt. Carmel enters the plain of Esdrachon

Migdal Eder: Hebrew, "tower of the flock," according to Alfred Edersheim in *The Life and Times of Jesus the Messiah, Vol. 1* (Longmans, Green & Co., 1884), pp. 186–187

Miletus: City of Roman province of Asia (Acts 20:15, 17)

Nahor: Proper name (Luke 3:34)

Obed bar Elihu: Fictional name made from Old Testament references meaning "Obed son of Elihu" (Luke 3:32)

Onesimus: Greek, "profitable"; proper name of central figure in the story recorded in Philemon, a runaway slave who became a Christian (Philemon 10)

Paraclete: Greek, "one called alongside" and "helper"; name for the Holy Spirit given by Jesus to his disciples

Pax Romana: Latin, "Roman Peace"; referencing the peaceful conditions produced by Roman military and civil forces

Philemon: Man addressed in Paul's New Testament letter of the same name; Paul's friend and owner of the slave Onesimus

Philippi: A chief city in proconsular Macedonia, named for the Father of Alexander the Great. The church there received Paul's letter.

Pneuma: Greek, "breath," "wind," and "Spirit of God"; used here for the role of the Paraclete

Quirinius: Governor of Syria when Caesar Augustus ordered the census that sent Joseph and Mary to Bethlehem (Luke 2:2)

Sanhedrin: Jewish religious council with some civil authority, composed of seventy elders, mostly aristocratic, presided over by a high priest (Numbers 11:16–24)

Shaloam: Hebrew, "peace," "wholeness," "tranquility," especially when used in relationship to God

Shaloam lechem: Hebrew greeting, literally "peace to you"

Talitha cum: Aramaic, "little girl"; also verbal imperative, "stand up," "arise" (Mark 5:41)

Tetelesthai: Greek, perfect passive tense of verb τελειω (*teleio*) meaning "finished," "completed," or "concluded"; Jesus's final word to his Father while on the cross

Theudas: Proper name (Acts 5:36)

Yeshua: Hebrew transliteration for the name "Jesus" (יֵשׁוּעַ)

Zebedee: Name of a family prominent in the New Testament; Zebedee is the father of the disciples James and John (Matthew 4:21, Mark 10:35, Luke 5:10)

About the Author

Kenneth Brown, a lifelong Texan, graduated from Howard Payne University in Brownwood, Texas in 1952 with a double major in English and Biblical Greek. He earned his Master's of Theology in Biblical Greek from Southwestern Baptist Seminary in 1959, and went on to study Educational Psychology at the University of Texas, Austin.

After serving as a Baptist pastor for fifty years, Brown retired and taught Bible study and biblical Greek at Trinity Baptist Church in Kerrville, Texas.

Brown lives in south Texas with his wife of over sixty-five years. They enjoy spending time with their five children, sixteen grandchildren, and many great-grandchildren.